I0365965

moon
D'Moon

Credit goes to
author O'Ceanic,
and the team of designers,
photographers, cartoonists,
and editors at the publisher: D'Moon

first edition: 2024
Quote Art: see book "Train of Morrow"

ISBN: 978-1-933187-32-7

Slight variations may occur
as part of the print-on-demand process
since each book is manufactured in its entirety.

Your feedback is most welcome ~
publisher@worldculturepictorial.com

游子远
远 AFAR
Random notes on road

Oceanic
d'moon books

Amazing! Half of world population can speak more than one language, that has inspired this book series, with Latin Alphabet English, and picture-word Chinese, two out of top three most spoken languages.

《aFar远》 is the first book in the series "random notes on road游子远".

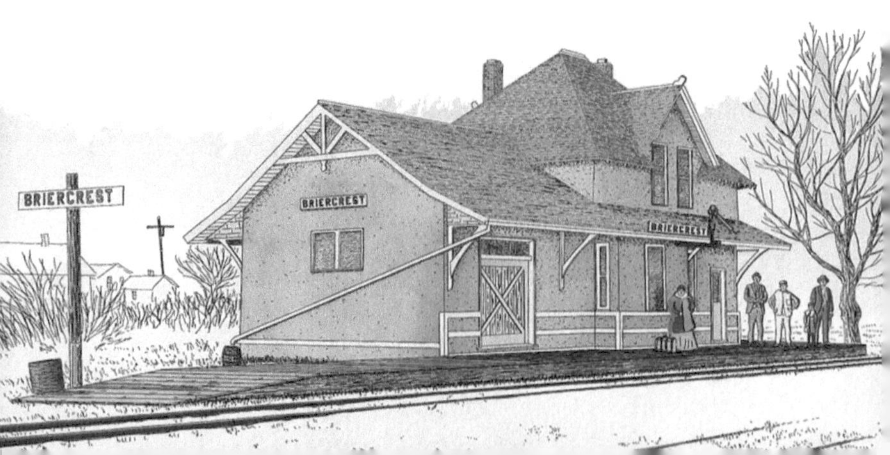
BRIERCREST
BRIERCREST
BRIERCREST

无论多遥远

吉祥

Latin Alphabet
and picture-words
are paired up,
no translation
but connections,
common notion
of Aristotle,
of LaoTsu,
of Shakespeare,
of LiBai, of SuDongpo...
Broad content spans
over thousands of years.

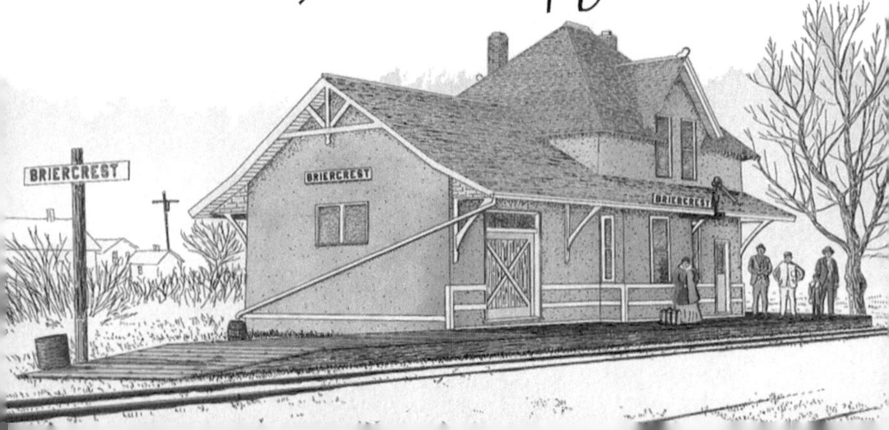
BRIERCREST
BRIERCREST
BRIERCREST

无论在何方

安
康

To quote Hugo: To learn to read is to light a fire; every syllable that is spelled out is a spark.

Train and book.
Notebook and pen.
See more. Read more.
A journey of learning.
A journey of growing wise.

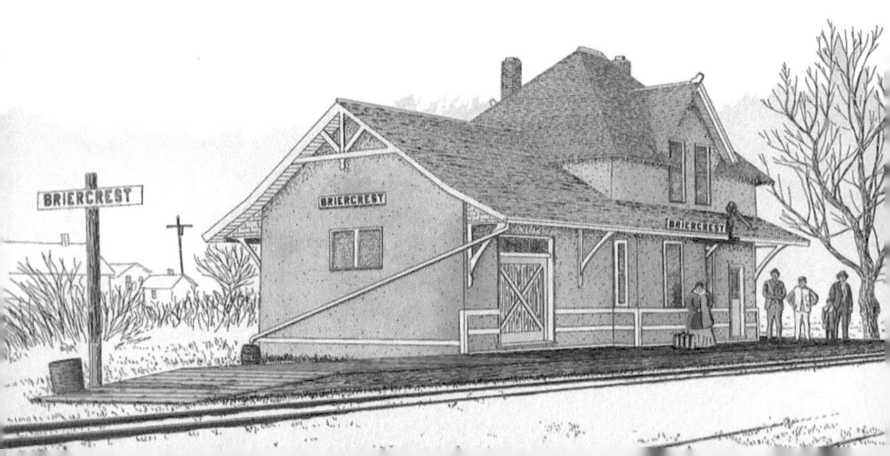
BRIERCREST
BRIERCREST
BRIERCREST

火车永恒的节奏中. 看着
一排排匆匆忙忙跑向后方
的是树木山丘平原江河,
一切源源无际,无始无端,
或许生命如此,
生活亦如此.
天涯海角.随读随笔以便
再读再学再悟.知识智慧
落在这里.点点滴滴, 由
远而近,如同远行的火车
置游子于自然中.

Good Luck!

o i o

9 out of 50 (LaoTsu)
happiness (Aristotle)
mind (Shakespeare)
the first (Aristotle)
guise (Honoré de Balzac)
harmony (Hugo)
bestowed (Plato)

吉祥安康

◦ i ◦

“上善若水”(老子)
儿远行,母担忧
百善孝为先
感天动地的爱心
100多个“孝”皇帝
慈念家和.唐宋600年
”微妙玄通”(老子)

Quote Art

◦ II ◦

stately style
restless
scale quivers
fate be led
soulful shadow
secret regret
in gloom
tears frozen
Let me be!

成语典故

◦ II ◦

三顾茅庐　(一至五)
六神无主　(六至十)
林栖谷隐　(木林森)
水滴石穿　(水冰淼)
日月穿梭　(日月朤)
品箫弄笛　(口回品)
由博返约　(田由雷)
丛雀渊鱼　(人从丛)

Wine and Poetry

◦ iii ◦

poetry, univeral
wine and snow
choice and destiny
sorrow in batallions
signs
best doctor, least medicine
so often
Know the answer, forget...

天高路远

○ iii ○

雨林古体诗首版

"善", the same
picture-word,
appears 9 times
in the 50-word
Chanper 8 of
LaoTsu's TaoTeJing,
most popular,
well read
next to the Bible.

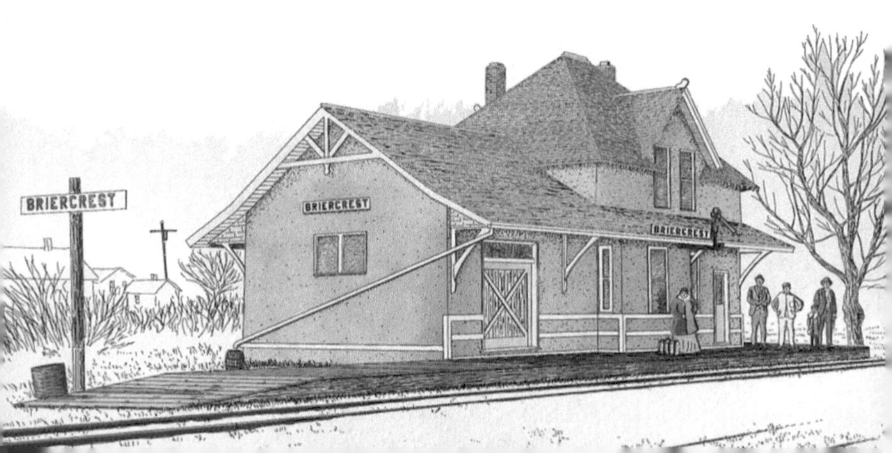
BRIERCREST
BRIERCREST

✦远✦游子远

上善若水。
水善利万物而不争，
处众人之所恶，
　故几于道。
居善地，心善渊，
与善仁，言善信，
政善治，事善能，
动善时。
夫唯不争，故无尤。
～老子「道德经」
第八章

Happiness is
the settling of the soul
into its most
appropriate spot.
~ Aristotle

The most sincere care
and love can
be felt by heart.

BRIERCREST
BRIERCREST
BRIERCREST

✦远✦游子运

儿远游，慈母泪

火车上有多少游子告别了恩重如山的老一辈,越来越远离了."游子未能归,感慨心如捣'古人的诗写了代代人的泪.

爱子心无尽，归家喜及辰。
寒衣针线密，家信墨痕新。
见面怜清瘦，呼儿问苦辛。
低徊愧人子，不敢叹风尘。
清　蒋士铨《岁暮到家》

人子孝顺心，岂在荣与槁？
昨宵天雨霜，江空岁华老。
游子未能归，感慨心如捣。
元·王冕<墨萱图》

Frame your mind
to mirth and
merriment which bars
a thousand harms
and lengthens life.
~ Shakespeare

BRIERCREST
BRIERCREST

百善孝为先

家喻户晓的名大忠臣包
丞相包公辞官7年侍奉
父母.宋仁宗赠予「孝
肃」.正如陆游《人生
堂堂七尺身》的诗句-
不欺当从一念始,
自古孝子为忠臣。

1057年，20岁的苏轼
与弟苏辙进京皆考中进
士.四月苏轼回乡为母
守孝三年后回京。
1066年父苏洵过世.苏
轼回蜀为父守孝三年。

Courage
is the first of
human virtues
because
it makes all others
possible.

~ Aristotle

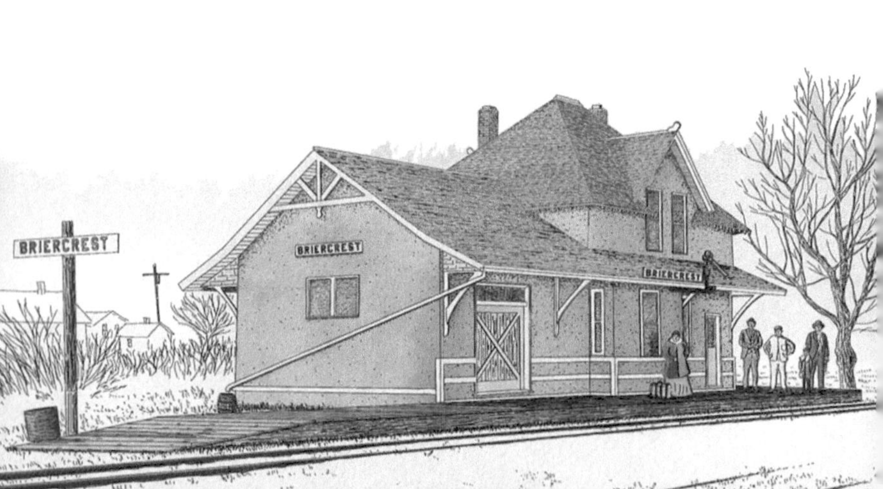
BRIERCREST
BRIERCREST
BRIERCREST

感天动地的爱心

大孝子江革乱世动荡时背着寡母四处逃难。途中多次遇到盗匪，见他对母亲一片孝心，都放他们一条生路。进城后，他靠着当佣人奉养母亲，自己省吃俭用。被皇帝封为谏议大夫

汉文帝刘恒在位24年以德治理天下，服伺三年卧病3年的母亲常常目不交睫、衣不解带

(*古代25孝子故事*)

It is our choice
of good or evil
that determines
our character,
not our opinion
about good or evil.
~ Aristotle

A mother's arms are
made of tenderness and
children sleep soundly
in them.

~ Victor Hugo

BRIERCREST
BRIERCREST
BRIERCREST

100多个"孝"皇帝

这里仅列出21位 -
孝惠皇帝 諱盈
太宗孝文皇帝 諱恆
孝景皇帝 諱啟
世宗孝武皇帝 諱徹
孝昭皇帝 諱拂陵
中宗孝宣皇帝 諱詢
高宗孝元皇帝 諱奭
孝成皇帝 諱鰲
孝哀皇帝 諱欣
孝平皇帝 諱衡

A mother's happiness
is like a beacon,
lighting up the future but
reflected also on the past
in the guise of
fond memories.

~ Honoré de Balzac

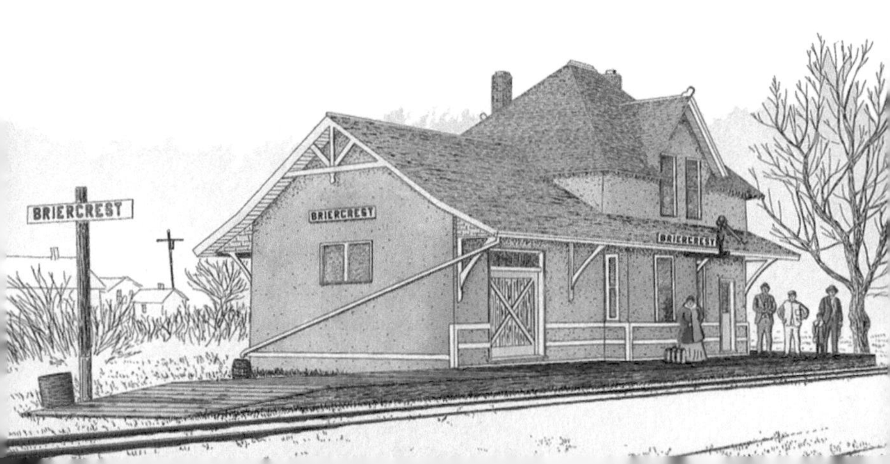
BRIERCREST
BRIERCREST
BRIERCREST

顯宗孝明皇帝　諱莊
肅宗孝章皇帝　諱炟
孝和皇帝　諱肇
孝殤皇帝　諱隆
恭宗孝安皇帝　諱祜
孝順皇帝　諱保
孝沖皇帝　諱炳
孝質皇帝　諱纘
孝桓皇帝　諱志
孝靈皇帝　諱宏
孝愍皇帝　諱協
(*古代有多少皇帝
被称为孝皇帝*)

Poetry is finer and
more philosophical
than history;
for poetry expresses
the universal.

~ Aristotle

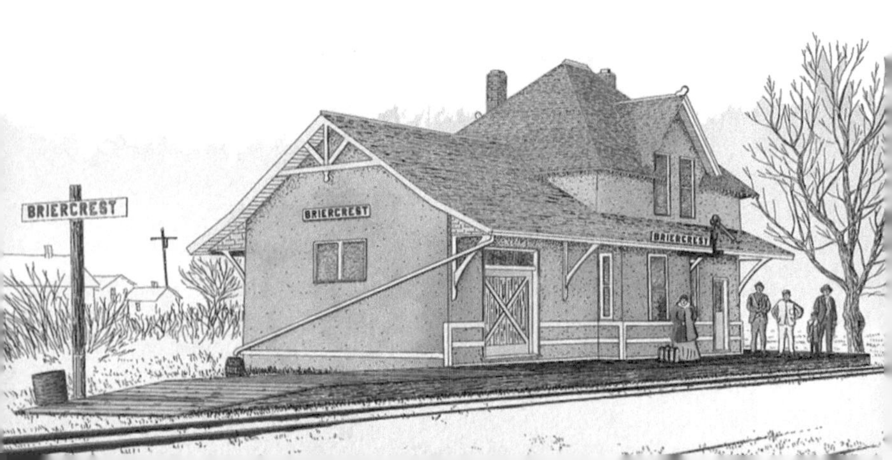
BRIERCREST
BRIERCREST
BRIERCREST

慈念家和。唐宋600年各朝代中孝皇帝比例最高是宋(18:17)唐(21:19).而且唐宋(618~1279年)两个朝代,600多年的传统文化给后人留下了举世闻名的大诗人及唐诗宋词。传统文化孝治天下.在诗词中可见一斑.李商隐《送母回乡》。路上"悲泪哽在喉"–

停车茫茫顾，困我成楚囚。
感伤从中起，悲泪哽在喉。
慈母方病重，欲将名医投。
车接今在急，天竟情不留！
母爱无所报，人生更何求！

To put everything
in balance is good,
to put everything
in harmony is better.

~ Victor Hugo

BRIERCREST

又如唐.孟郊的《游子吟》
慈母手中线，游子身上衣。
临行密密缝，意恐迟迟归。
谁言寸草心，报得三春晖。

"爱子心无尽";
"人子孝顺心"

善善相报。
家和万事兴。
莫非由此唐朝宋朝600年
大诗人倍出？
(*孝皇帝比例最高者*)

Kindness
which is bestowed
on the good
is never lost.

~ Plato

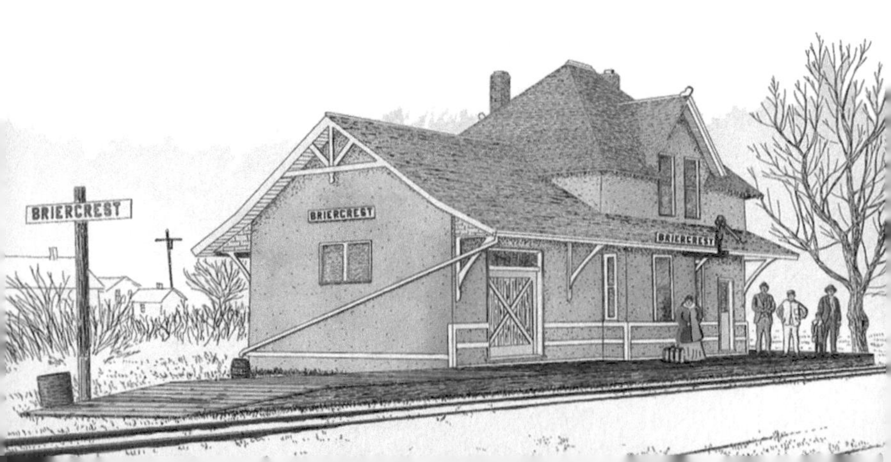
BRIERCREST
BRIERCREST
BRIERCREST

"微妙玄通"(老子)

老子言，
"古之善为道者，
微妙玄通，
深不可识.「道德经」

"善为道"，
启悟人生的灯
点亮了几千年。

quote "visit my confidant"
to introduce the poem

(No noise, be silent)
My step is cautioned
Not to intrude,
Not to disturb,
the forever grand,
stately mood
of each
redwood.

火车不紧不慢，时不时鸣叫地前进。窗外如同陶渊明对

“智者乐山山如画，

仁者乐水水无涯”

列车窗内时不时地看到带愁容的面孔“人生是逆行，我亦是行人”（苏东坡），有谁的生活中不曾有悲伤，没有忧愁？对窗外凝视了一阵，视线转会书笔记本...

quote "a cottage"
to introduce the poem

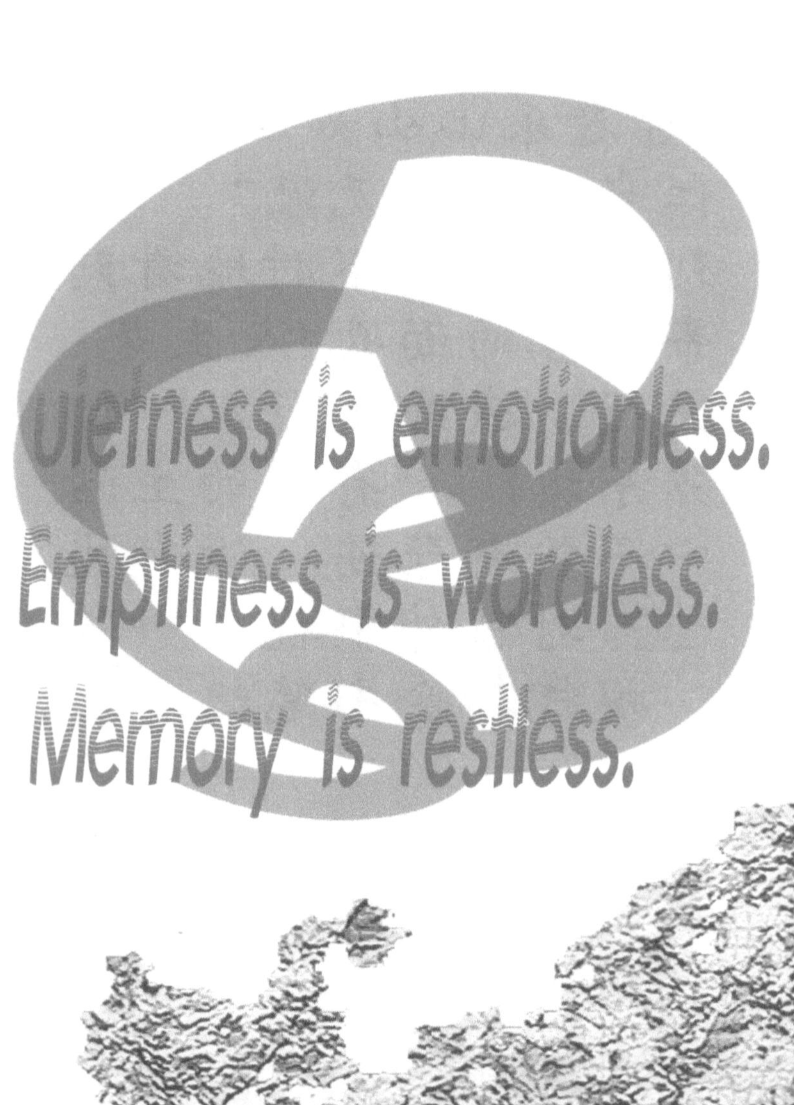
uietness is emotionless.
Emptiness is wordless.
Memory is restless.

一　　一言九鼎

二　　二一添作五

三　　三顾茅庐

四　　四两拨千斤

五　　五谷丰登

quote "Mercy! my Lord of Fame"
to introduce the poem

Future
spells uncertainty.
What should I do?
...
The scale
quivers.
Reason
runs
out of Sense.

六　　六神无主

七　　七上八下

八　　八仙过海

九　　九九归一

十　　十之八九

quote "have we ever met" to introduce the poem

Have
we ever met
or not acquainted yet
Who's
spinning the thread
Where'll our fate be led

沐　沐雨梳风

木　木已成舟

林　林栖谷隐

森　森罗万象

杰　地灵人杰

quote "a little sad shadow" to introduce the poem

A Little spots,
round and shallow,
Scatter over the snow.
Footprints loyally follow
The soulful, tiny shadow.

水　　水滴石穿
　　　滴水之恩
泉　　　当涌泉相报
冰　　冰冻三尺
　　　　非一日之寒
淼　　淼淼烟波

quote "secret regret"
to introduce the poem

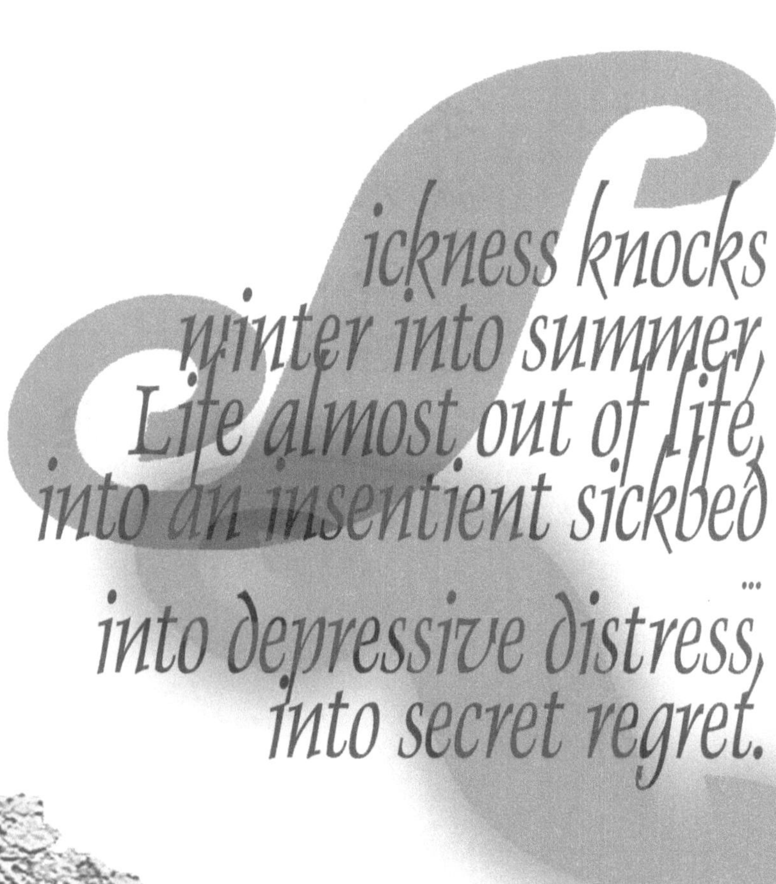

Sickness knocks
winter into summer,
Life almost out of life,
into an insentient sickbed
...
into depressive distress,
into secret regret.

日　　日月穿梭
月　　日月丽天
朋　　前程朋朋
日　　日新月异
月　　日积月累
明　　明日复明日

quote "so long"
to introduce the poem

Emotion takes off into storm -
The ocean of clouds is in gloom..

...

mingling Future and Past,
twisting Love and Lust,
meandering Affection's trek,
melting Rationale's legs.

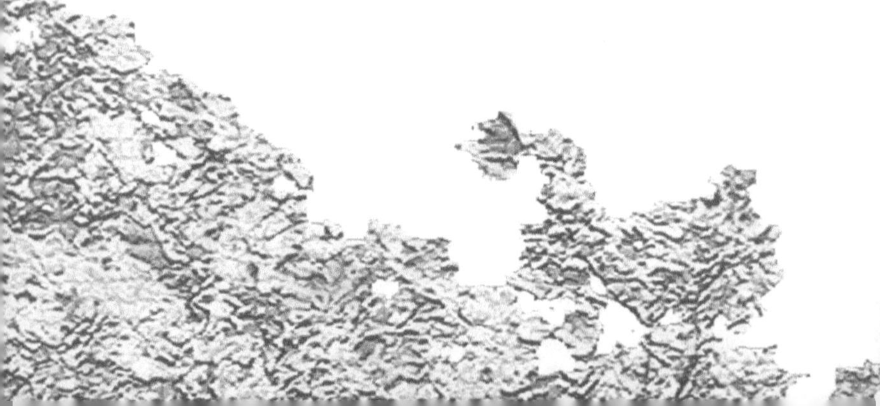

口　　口若悬河

吕　　吕端大事

　　　不糊涂

古　　古往今来

如　　如履薄冰

回　　回眸一笑

品　　品箫弄笛

quote "weeping sky"
to introduce the poem

Deep into midnight, cry
in soundless silence. Sky
is weeping,
tears falling so slow
frozen
into crystal snow
to quiet down
the ground
in dark, laying
mourning white

田　　田月桑时
雷　　雷厉风飞
由　　由博返约
甲　　甲乙丙丁
里　　里里外外
果　　果如其言

quote "Mercy! my Lord of Fame"
to introduce the poem

D
ream of Glory –
unhand me!
Leave me be!
Mercy!
My Lord of Fame.

人　　人非圣贤
　　　　孰能无过
从　　从从容容
丛　　丛雀渊鱼
众　　众口难调
个　　个中滋味
大　　大笔如椽
天　　天不变
　　　　道亦不变

A deep below the deep, And
a height beyond the height!
Our hearing is not hearing,
And our seeing is not sight.

~ Alfred Lord Tennyson

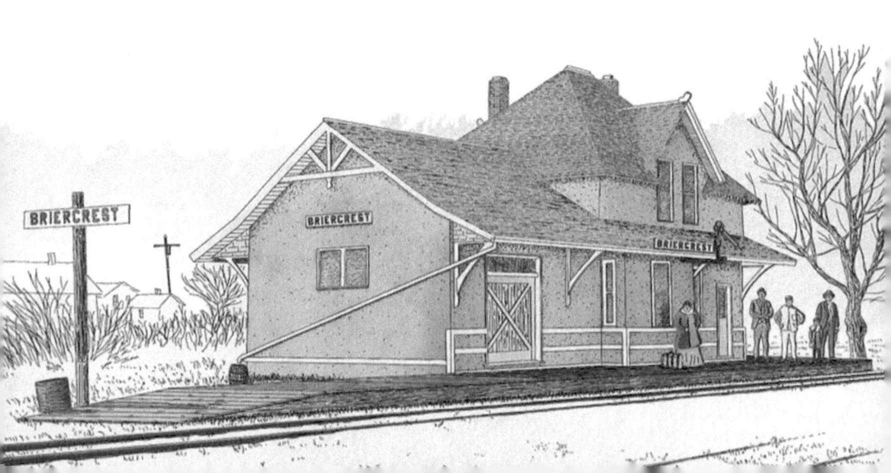
BRIERCREST
BRIERCREST
BRIERCREST

列车铿锵有力地前进，乌云密布的天空渐渐地远去了.窗外是平原，山林，小木屋.草地青青，几头沉稳的牛...看上去不紧不慢悠哉悠.”别有天地非人间”恰如李白对’何意栖碧山’的回答.李白,诗仙,酒仙.自然和诗，诗和酒似乎有不解之缘

I love everything
that is old; old friends,
old times, old manners,
old books, old wines.

~ Oliver Goldsmith

To appreciate
the beauty of a snowflake,
it is necessary
to stand out in the cold.

~ Aristotle

BRIERCREST
BRIERCREST
BRIERCREST

雨林✦八言诗

《雪寒酒暖》

夜暗星闪今非去年
前书后书忧系诗篇
昔日话别天涯十载
雪寒星寒杯孤酒暖

Excellence is
never an accident.
It is always the result of
high intention,
sincere effort, and
intelligent execution; it
represents the wise choice
of many alternatives -
choice, not chance,
determines your destiny.
~ Aristotle

BRIERCREST
BRIERCREST
BRIERCREST

雨林✦十五字词

《问墨》

浩然正气
问墨挥笔
运筹万里
惊天地

When sorrows come,
they come
not single spies,
but in battalions.
~ Shakespeare

Give me
a bowl of wine,
In this I bury all
unkindness.
~ Shakespeare

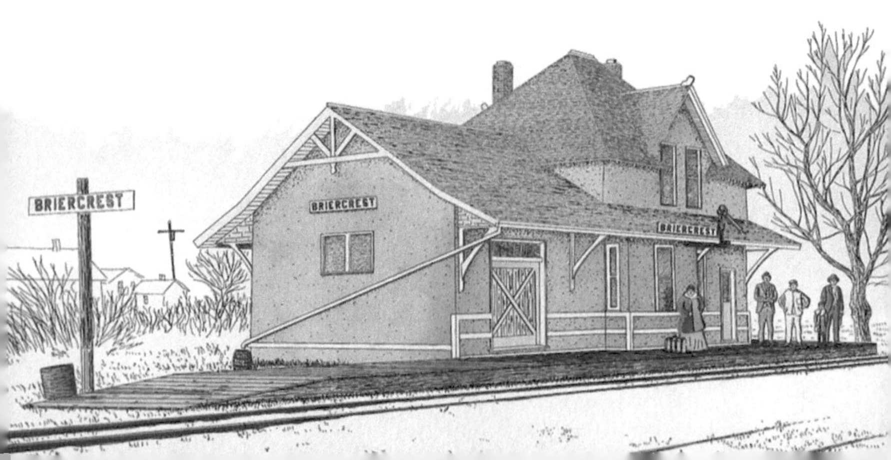
BRIERCREST
BRIERCREST

雨林✦八言诗

《回回梦醒》

弃笔父从义赴疆场
抚独子母泪守空房
娘苦中苦儿刚中钢
漫漫黑夜领歌牢房
昂首四方忠烈栋梁
路坎坷远游落他乡
书扬名却难驱凄凉
回回梦醒哭喊爹娘

He that is thy friend indeed,
He will help thee in thy need:
If thou sorrow, he will weep;
If thou wake, he cannot sleep:
Thus of every grief in heart
He with thee does bear a part.
These are certain signs
to know Faithful friend
from flattering foe.

~ Shakespeare

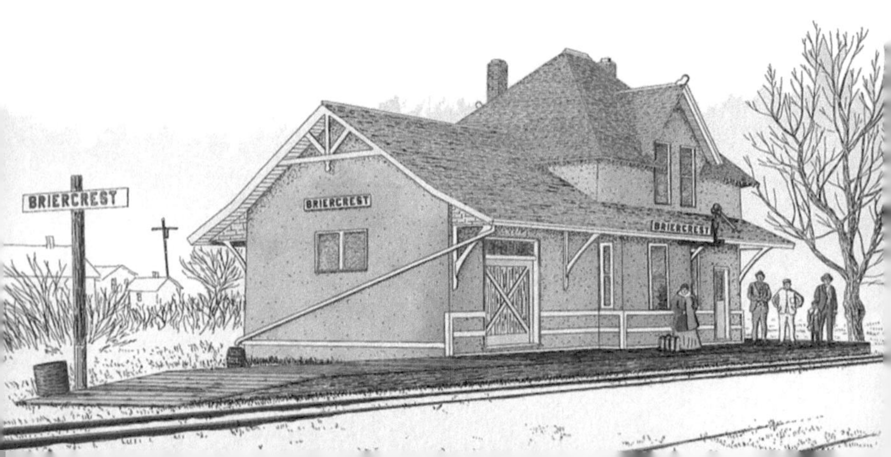
BRIERCREST
BRIERCREST

雨林✦八言诗

《莫慌》

骤然风狂水啸浪吼
翻转乾坤翻转小舟
骤然骤然天逝地没
莫慌莫慌定魂定魄
舟飞舟落定风定波
海水泪水苍天怜我

Wine is sunlight
held together by water.

~ Galileo

The best doctor gives
the least medicines.

~ Benjamin Franklin

BRIERCREST
BRIERCREST
BRIERCREST

雨林✦八言诗

《华佗再现》

七尺男儿白衣披挂
才华诚爱行路潇洒
华佗问世若隐若现
恒星眨眼回我问话

I drink to your health
when I'm with you,
my friend,
I drink to your health
when I'm alone,
I drink to your health
so often,
I'm starting to
worry about my own!

~ Irish Proverb

BRIERCREST
BRIERCREST
BRIERCREST

雨林✦七言诗

《思念》

白云蘑菇蔚蓝天
客笑斟满再斟满
几问潋潋葡萄酒
知否思念绕心头

Wine is the answer,
but I do not remember
the question.

~ Irish Proverb

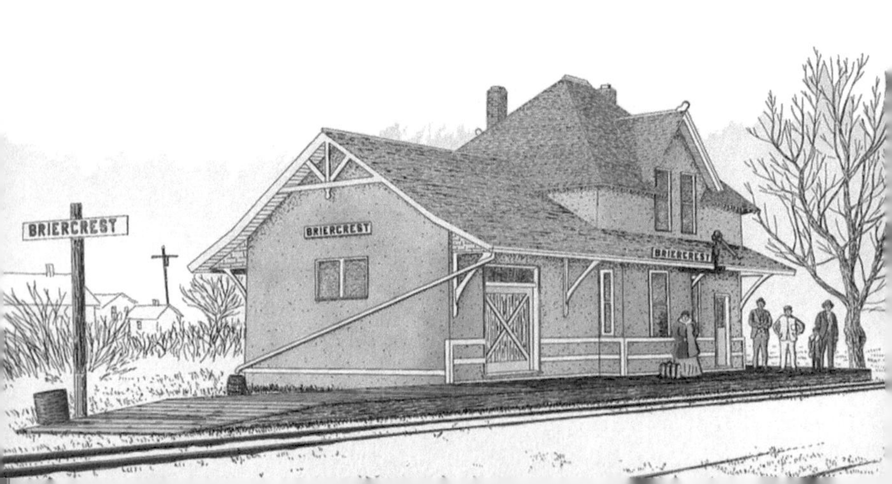
BRIERCREST
BRIERCREST
BRIERCREST

雨林✦五言诗

《静》

窗外绿葱葱
细雨落无声
闹市心无尘
古今走笔锋

www.ingramcontent.com/pod-product-compliance
Lightning Source LLC
Chambersburg PA
CBHW060540080526
44586CB00012B/805

9781933187327